Anonymous

Observations on Mr. Dundas's India Budget

Anonymous

Observations on Mr. Dundas's India Budget

ISBN/EAN: 9783337059132

Printed in Europe, USA, Canada, Australia, Japan

Cover: Foto ©Suzi / pixelio.de

More available books at **www.hansebooks.com**

OBSERVATIONS

ON.

Mr. DUNDAS's

INDIA BUDGET.

LONDON:

Printed for J. DEBRETT, oppofite Burlington
Houfe, Piccadilly.

M. DCC. XC.

THE Public are much obliged to Mr. Tierney, for his propofition to defer the reports of the refolutions moved by Mr. Dundas, until after the recefs, becaufe it gives us an opportunity of candidly examining the affertions on both fides the Houfe.

This is the fourth year that Mr. Dundas has laid before the Houfe of Commons a general view of the finances and government of India; and although the prefent account is confeffedly more favourable than that of any former year, the ftock has fallen, and is now confiderably below all other government fecurities.

B   My

My object is not so much to inquire into the cause of this depreſſion of the Company's ſtock, as to examine ſuch repreſentations of both ſides of the Houſe, as in my opinion are contrary to truth.

In Bengal, it appears, that there was a ſurplus of two millions, five hundred, and thirty-ſix thouſand pounds, after the payment of all the expences of the laſt year ; and that by the eſtimate tranſmitted by Lord Cornwallis, a ſurplus exceeding the laſt by ten thouſand pounds, may be expected in the preſent year.

Of the propriety and policy of continuing this ſurplus at ſo great a height, Mr. Dundas expreſſed ſome doubts.

With reſpect to the revenue ariſing in Bengal from land, it ſeems to be allowed, by Mr. Dundas, that there is no reaſon to believe it will at any time decreaſe : on the contrary, ſome of the beſt informed men, who have been in India, are of opinion, that

it

it will admit of a confiderable increafe without oppreffion.

But there is another great article of revenue, the falt, which in the laft year produced a profit of above eight hundred thoufand pounds, and is eftimated to produce as much in the prefent. This is generally fuppofed to be a very ferious oppreffion, and therefore. I fhall confider it a little at large.

Mr. Francis was a Member of the Supreme Council when the plan was formed by Mr. Haftings, in 1780, for managing this great branch of the public revenue. He oppofed it, and fo did Mr. Barwell, and Mr. Wheler; but *not* from an idea that it would be an oppreffion; *they conceived, that it would endanger the fcanty revenue, which the Company at that time drew from falt.* At length they agreed, to a partial adoption of the plan, on the feparate refponfibility of Mr. Haftings. It fucceeded fo well, that in a few months the Board *unanimoufly* confented to an extenfion of it; and then the fyftem was formed, *which has continued ever fince.* The utmoft that Mr. Haf-

tings

tings propofed to raife from the people for this article, was half a million fterling a-year; and he gave it, as his decided opinion, that fuch a fum might be raifed without oppreffion, or injuftice. It has, however, increafed, until the net profit in the laft, and the prefent year, is above eight hundred thoufand pounds.

That the increafed population of Bengal and Bahar can bear no proportion to fuch an increafed confumption, in fo fhort a time, is clear. Indeed, all reafoning upon it is out of the queftion : for the Company laft year fold their falt in Calcutta thirty per cent. higher than they did when Mr. Haftings, and Sir John Macpherfon were in the government; and, therefore, be the population more or lefs, it muft come to the poor at a very heavy, and an oppreffive price. But with a confiderable re- duction in the price, it will afford a noble re- venue; and that revenue muft neceffarily increafe, with an increafed population.

Mr. James Grant, who held a very im- portant office under the government of Sir John Macpherfon, proved, to the fatisfaction
of

of the East-India Company from authentic documents, that the confumption of falt in Bengal in the year 1780 was confiderably more than one third beyond the confumption in 1765. He adds, " a lapfe of fifteen " years under the lenity of the Englifh Go- " vernment, had certainly operated a very " material change in the ftate of things; " greater fecurity and freedom in agricul- " ture, manufactures, and commerce, in- " creafed confiderably the population of the " country, with the wealth and profperity " of its inhabitants : an additional confump- " tion of all the neceffaries of life was a na- " tural confequence, and fully evinced the " improved condition of the Britifh pro- " vinces."

Mr. Grant then carries his view down from the year 1780 to 1787, and adds, that the farther increafe in the confumption of falt in the latter period " indicates, with moral, in- " fallible certainty, a prodigious increafe of " population, and all its concomitant advan- " tages, in a period of little more than twen- " ty years."

I

Such

Such is the reprefentation of Mr. Grant, a gentleman who is now in England, and who means, as I am informed, to publifh to the world, his remarks upon the revenues of Bengal.

Mr. Dundas thinks that one hundred and fifty, or two hundred thoufand pounds may be fubtracted from the falt revenue, but that the furplus will ftill be the fame, becaufe he can reduce eftablifhments at Madras and Bombay to that amount. If patronage to minifters at the expence of the Eaft-India Company be given up, I am confident that a reduction to the amount at leaft of half a million a year may take place at thofe fettlements.

Of the land revenues of Bengal and Benares, which are the great and material articles, Mr. Francis did not feem to doubt, and he expreffed his fatisfaction that they were likely to be permanently fixed. In point of fact, they have varied very little for many years, and for the laft ten years have been remarkably equal.

Mr.

Mr. Francis finding that the price of falt varied in this laft year from three hundred to feven hundred rupees the hundred maund, fuppofed the latter to be the felling price ; and making his calculations upon that ground, and fuppofing every native in Bengal to confume one ounce a day, which is double what he eats, and fuppofing a family of five perfons to live upon the labour of one man, which is never the cafe, very fairly concluded, that this muft be a moft grievous oppreffion, and that the natives muft have recourfe to fome deftructive fubftitute for falt : but he knows that the evil was immediately corrected ; and he muft know, that falt fold in Calcutta at three hundred rupees the hundred maunds, will afford a very great revenue to the Company, and that the natives can then purchafe it upon fair terms.

The inftance he brought of Lord Clive's monopoly, will not bear him out in the leaft. If his Lordfhip had made the Eaft-India Company the *principals*, Mr. Bolts would have written againft him in vain ; but the fact was this—an opinion prevailed in England,

land, that the war with Coffim Ally Cawn had in a great meafure been occafioned by the private trade of the Company's fervants: Lord Clive was particularly inftructed to regulate the trade in falt, beetle nut, and tobacco, in conjunction with the Nabob. His Lordfhip procured the fovereignty of Bengal for the Company, in fact, though not in name. He then determined to take the *whole* trade in falt into the hands *of the Company's fervants*, to be managed by a committee for *their benefit*, referving a duty to the Company ; and he particularly provided, that falt fhould not be fold in Calcutta beyond a given price, two hundred rupees the hundred maunds. Mr. Bolts wrote a very falfe and inflammatory account of this bufinefs. The nation revolted at the idea of monopolizing fo material a neceffary of life, *for the benefit of individuals*, and the fociety was abolifhed : but the land upon which falt is manufactured is as much the property of the Company as the land that produces rice ; they have as much right to raife a revenue from the one as from the other, and Mr. Francis *fully approved of the plan by which the*

the present revenue is raised. It is the duty of Government to take care that the price is kept within proper bounds ; and that done, it is, in fact, the only article from which any material revenue can be raised in Bengal, the land excepted ; and it has this advantage, *that it must increase with an increased population.*

I shall now follow Mr. Dundas and Mr. Francis to another subject.

The former expatiated very fully upon the improved and improving state of Bengal, and took, a little unreasonably I confess, credit *to government and to Lord Cornwallis for it.* I am not disposed to withhold, either from the one or the other, what is justly their due.

Mr. Dundas has the merit of agreeing with the Directors, in fixing their civil establishments in Bengal upon an œconomical footing; and Lord Cornwallis has the merit of obeying their orders. Though Sir John Macpherson had the heaviest part of the task to go through.

C   But

But as to the revenues, *they are conducted in the same manner, and they continue at the same amount* as they did, when Lord Cornwallis arrived there, and for many years before, the falt revenue excepted, which it is generally agreed produces 200,000l. a-year *more than it ought to do.*

Mr. Francis laid very particular ftrefs, and I really think, in fome places, with a good deal of reafon, upon a letter from Lord Cornwallis, dated the 2d of Auguft laft. The letter has been much the fubject of converfation in all companies; nor do I know how to reconcile it to other letters, which Lord Cornwallis has fent in the fame year; even taking it as Mr. Dundas defires us, with its context.

The firft thing to confider, is the fubject upon which this letter was written.

The Directors fent orders to Lord Cornwallis in the year 1786, to let the lands in Bengal for ten years, as preparatory to a *permanent unalterable fettlement.* This plan was found,

found, upon clofer infpection, to be attended, with fo many difficulties, that it required three years to collect materials ; nor is the plan, as far as we know, at this moment adopted.

Lord Cornwallis refers to papers in order to fhew *the principles* on which the plan is founded, and therefore he thinks it *unneceffary* to ftate them in his letter.

But the papers to which his Lordfhip refers, are certainly very defective. In the very firft outline of the plan, as far as I can trace it, there is a difficulty which I fhould have thought could not eafily have been got over. Government, upon the prefent fyftem, demands from a Zemindar a revenue of ten thoufand rupees, as the full rent he is to pay. The Zemindar declines to pay fo much. The land is then let to a farmer, and the Zemindar has his mofhaira for his fubfiftence. This happens every day. The next year the Zemindar may agree to the terms of government, and he then enjoys his right ; but in the event of a *permanent* fettlement, if the

Ze-

Zemindar *refuses* to comply with the terms of government, he is difpoffeffed, and *can never be reftored.* This is but one of a thoufand difficulties which will occur; though I am well aware that at firft view nothing appears fo eafy as to fix a permanent fettlement; and it has been a favourite idea with Mr. Haftings and Mr. Francis, and with their refpective fupporters, to let the lands upon leafes for lives.* But

---

* Suppofing the revenues in Bengal that arife from land, to be in the nature of a land tax in England; it is certainly eafy to fay, that the land tax fhall be fixed and unalterable; but a Zemindar, who is the higheft order of landholders in India, cannot be compared to a freeholder in Great Britain. The following is the moft accurate defcription of a Zemindar I have ever met with; the writer of it is one of the ableft amongft the Company's fervants in Bengal. I am fure no one can read it without being convinced, that we cannot argue from any thing we know in England, of the tenure of landed property in India.

" For my own part, from all the proofs I have hither-
" to feen adduced, refpecting the rights of Zemindars,
" I do not agree with Mr. Law in thinking them pro-
" prietors of the foil, and the Ryott but a vaffal or te-
" nant; if he ufes the terms *proprietor* and *tenant* in
" their common acceptation; as I do not conceive
" the

But I entirely agree with Mr. Francis, that the expectations of *increase of revenue* which are held out from this plan, *are in the highest degree fallacious*; that is to say, whatever future

" the Zemindar was at liberty to let out his lands to
" the greatest advantage for himself, as seems essen-
" tial to the general idea of *land property*; or that he
" can dispossess the Ryott after long occupancy;
" which implies a privilege not possessed, I believe,
" by the persons usually denominated by the term
" *tenants.*

" The Zemindar appears to me to be a landholder
" of a peculiar description, not defineable by any sin-
" gle term in our language. A collector of the re-
" venues of the state from the cultivator, allowed to
" succeed to the land, composing his Zemindary by
" inheritance; yet, in general, required to take out a
" renewal of his title from the sovereign or his repre-
" sentative; permitted to transfer his Zemindary by
" sale, or gift; yet commonly obliged to obtain pre-
" vious special permission. Privileged to be generally
" the annual contractor of the public revenue, re-
" ceivable from his Zemindary; yet set aside with a
" provision for his maintenance, whenever it was the
" pleasure of government to collect the revenue by
" separate agency; authorized in Bengal since the
" early part of the present century, to apportion in the
" Pur-

future increafe may refult from increafed
population, *would take place, whether the plan
were adopted or not.*

, Lord

" Purgunnahs, villages, and lefler divifions of lands
" within his Zemindary, the abwab, or affeffment, im-
" pofed by the Soubadar, ufually in fome proportion
" to the ftandard of the Jumma of the Zemindary,
" eftablifhed by Turunmull and others ; yet fubject
" to the difcretional interference of government,
" either to equalize the amount affeffed on par-
" ticular divifions, or to abolifh what appeared op-
" preffive to the Ryott ; entitled to any contingent
" emolument proceeding from his contract, during
" the period of his agreement ; yet bound by the
" terms of his tenures, to deliver in a faithful ac-
" count of his receipts, refponfible by the fame terms
" for keeping the peace within his jurifdiction, and
" punifh the refractory ; yet apparently allowed to
" apprehend only, and deliver over to a Muffulman
" magiftrate for trial and punifhment.

" This is, in abftract, my prefent idea of a Zemin-
" dar, under the Mogul conftitution and practice ;
" and I have not formed my opinion haftily, I have
" read with attention Mr. Shore's able minute on the
" fubject, Mr. Grant's elaborate and praife-worthy
" analyfis, and the publifhed opinions of Meffrs.
" Haftings and Francis, defervedly held in confider-
" able

Lord Cornwallis fays, that the certainty which each individual will *now* feel, of being allowed to enjoy the fruits of his own labours, muft operate uniformly as incitements to exertion and induftry.

In

" able eftimation, not omitting the reports of the
" Committee of revenue in March 1786. It would,
" as I have already faid, fill a volume to explain my
" reafons for affenting to, or diffenting from, the op-
" pofite fentiments contained in thefe papers refpec-
" tively; although, therefore, a confcioufnefs of my
" inferiority would incline me to ftate the grounds
" of my own opinions, I am compelled at prefent to
" decline it."

Mr. Law, in a letter to the board of revenue, dated the 9th of January, 1788, fays, " I have in vain en-
" deavoured to find the Hindoo Synoname for the
" Perfian name Zemindar, and confequently failed in
" obtaining a diftinct account of his *tenure*, and rights;
" indeed under a feudal fyftem, which has prevailed from
" time immemorial, the idea of a quit or mocurery
" tenure *cannot have been entertained*; for the European
" maxim of keeping a diftinct military force, and of
" raifing fupplies by funding, *is totally unknown*. In-
" dependence and fecurity from arbitrary power was
" never claimed; *to affert it even, was tantamount to*
" *rebellion*.

" The

Is it admitted that property is *now* infe-
cure, or that it has been fo during the Britifh
government in Bengal?

Mr. Francis fuppofes that Mr. Shore, and
not Lord Cornwallis, wrote this letter. I
make no fuch fuppofition; but undoubtedly
the principal part of Lord Cornwallis's knowledge of the revenues, *he derives from Mr.
Shore*; and it is a fingular circumftance, that
from the fame fource *Mr. Francis derived his
information alfo.* The latter fent home a plan
in 1776, which it is well known was drawn
up by Mr. Shore and Mr. Ducarell. It con-
tains much ufeful information. But the main
fcope of Mr. Francis was to perfuade the Company, *that the lands in Bengal were let too
high*, and that there ought to be a deduction
of ten per cent. on all the rents. Without
fuch a deduction, Mr. Francis foretold *the*

"The *Marajahs*, under the Hindoo government,
"taxed his vaffals as his neceffities or partialities dic-
"tated. The Muffelman government obferved the
"fame principles; and when refractory Zemindars
"refufed to pay the tribute, the Emperor gave the
"eftate to a favourite officer, who was to repay him-
"felf the expence of fubduing it from the produce."

very

very speedy ruin of Bengal; but he well knows, that from 1776, to this time, the revenues have continued the same; or if there has been a difference, they are rather higher, and with this addition, that in so far as the price of salt is higher now, than it was in 1776, *so much more revenue has been drawn from the poor.*

Mr. Shore, the supposed author of the two letters, affirmed in the year 1781, " that " the natives were happier, and their proper- " ty better secured under our government, " than under that of their former sovereigns." This, he adds, " I speak *with all the confidence conviction inspires.*" How can this be reconciled to the apparent sense of Lord Cornwallis's letter.

The real meaning of Lord Cornwallis is this, that by the new plan, the natives will have that sort of *property in the land,* which they have not at present, *nor never had at any former period.* He is to form a *new constitution.*

For several years it was the practice in Bengal to make an annual settlement. of the

D land

lands—invariably fo, during the adminiftration of Mahomed Reza Cawn. The Directors, and the Board of controul, in fpeaking of
an annual fettlement, fay, " that it has in ma-
" ny points been impolitic and prejudicial."
They add, " For this we impute no blame to
" our Governor General, and Council, as
" your fentiments on this fubject were very
" wifely and fairly ftated to us in your general
" letter of the 10th of January, 1780."

No man wifhes more fincerely than I do,
that the adoption of the new plan may produce
every good confequence that Lord Cornwallis
hopes for from it.

His Lordfhip conceives it to be of the utmoft importance, that the principal landholders and traders fhould be *reftored* to fuch
circumftances, as to enable them to fupport
their families with decency. *That a regular
gradation of ranks* may be fupported, which
is no where more neceffary, than in Bengal,
for preferving order in civil fociety.

I lived many years in Bengal, and fome of
them under what was called the country government

vernment. Moſt undoubtedly there was then
a gradation of ranks amongſt the Mahometans,
which does not exiſt at the preſent day ; but
the reaſon is obvious ; Moorſhedabad was at
that time the ſeat of government. The Nabob of Bengal had then forty-five lacks of rupees a-year ; Mahomed Riza Cawn had nine
lacks ; there was a Fouzdar in every diſtrict ;
every revenue office was held by a native.
Many Mahometans of rank, ſince deceaſed,
had jaghires. The Mahometans are naturally
fond of pomp and expence, and all the money they received was circulated in the country. But I was told, that I could form a
very faint idea of the ſplendor of the government under the native ſovereigns, from what
I then ſaw ; yet the maſs of the people were
at that time juſt as poor as they are now ;
not ſo happy, as Mr. Shore ſays, nor their
property, whatever it was, ſo well ſe-
cured.

Since that period, a very great and impor-
tant change has taken place. The ſtipend of
the Nabob is reduced to ſixteen lacks of rupees a-year. The government is entirely ad-

D 2   admiminiftered by the Englifh ; and Calcutta has increafed in fize and confequence in a greater degree than Moorfhedabad has declined. A very long and expenfive war, chiefly fupported from Bengal, occafioned the extraction of immenfe fums in fpecie. The reftoration of peace *brought no relief to Bengal.* The revenues of that kingdom, Bahar, and Benares, with the amount of the Oude fubfidy, are above five millions fterling. Her expences for army, civil eftablifhments, ftipends, penfions, collections, &c. are about three millions ; and eighty lacks more are expended for inveftment. The balance is chiefly employed in paying the intereft of the debt in India, in remittances to China, and in fupporting the armies in the Carnatic and Bombay.

I believe I may venture to affirm, that there never was a government under Heaven, that has fubfifted fo many years under a fyftem fo deftructive ; and which has not only fubfifted, *but has actually flourifhed.*

The wifeft man who has confidered the fubject, cannot pretend to fay from what

fources

fources Bengal has been enabled to fupply the immenfe drains of treafure that it has fuftained for the thirty laft years. Mr. Francis's arguments carried this conviction to my mind in 1776, that the country could not go on without a change of fyftem; yet fince that period, the greateft exertions have been made in Bengal;* and we have the affurance of Lord Cornwallis, that this nation may depend upon the *continuance* of a furplus of more than two millions fterling a-year.

In another paragraph, Lord Cornwallis fays, that agriculture and internal commerce have for many years been *gradually* declining; that except Shroffs and Banians, the inhabitants of thefe provinces *were* advancing *haftily* to a general ftate of poverty and wretchednefs. Almoft every Zemindar is included in this defcription, which, though partly occafioned by their own indolence and extravagance, muft be attributed in a great

* The fupplies to Madras and Bombay, fince 1776, amount to above ten millions fterling, and the inveftments to Europe in the fame period exceed that fum.

meafure

meafure to the defects of our *former* fyftem of management.

Upon this paragraph Mr. Francis very juftly obferved, that *were* fhould be changed to *are*, fince, in point of fact, Lord Cornwallis had done nothing to avert the mifchief. *He* raifed the fame revenue; *He* fent the fame fupplies to Madras, Bombay, and China; *He* let the lands to farmers, when zemindars would not pay what Government demanded. In fhort, his Lordfhip in foreign and domeftic policy followed *precifely* the fyftem of his predeceffor, Sir John Macpherfon; who in like manner continued the fyftem of his predeceffor, Mr. Haftings.

That a great and material change has taken place in Bengal fince the Englifh acquired the fovereignty of that country, I allow: but it is a change that was inevitable, as muft ftrike every gentleman who has ever beftowed a thought upon the nature of government.

Bengal is a rich, extenfive, and commercial kingdom. Europe poured its treafures

2 into

into her lap, in exchange for her manufactures. From the Persian Gulph and the Red Sea she received bullion also. From Dehli, and the northern parts of Indostan, she had a return of wealth beyond what she paid in tribute to the Mogul. Much of the country was granted in jaghire. The jaghiredars lived upon their estates in a style beyond that of the first nobility of Great Britain. Such *was* the state of Bengal in the memory of many gentlemen now living; but a few years produced a very material alteration. The total destruction of the Persian empire annihilated her export trade to the Gulphs, and cut off one source of returning wealth. The invasion of Nadir Shah, the rebellions and massacres at Dehli, and in the northern provinces, destroyed another. The acquisition of Bengal by the English stopped the exportation of specie from Europe. The administration of government by the English themselves prevented that circulation of treasure, which was the consequence of every public office being held by the natives. Under the government that now exists, how could there be a *gradation of ranks?* From
the

the earlieſt accounts of time, there is not an inſtance of a government ſo *monſtruous* as that of the Engliſh in Bengal—I mean, where a government has been adminiſtered by a few people for the benefit of a *nation* at the diſtance of twelve thouſand miles *from the people governed.* In this ſenſe, what Mr. Burke once ſaid is ſtrictly true, that our government is in its beſt ſtate, a grievance.

We raiſe, or at leaſt we hope to raiſe, in England, one million a year beyond our expences. This money is laid out in decreaſing our debt, and for the benefit of the nation. In Bengal we raiſe above two millions beyond our expences—do we conſider for a moment about laying out that money for the advantage of Bengal? Certainly not. We lay a part of it out in inveſtment, becauſe *England* wants muſlins. We ſend large ſums to China, becauſe *England* wants tea. We ſend half a million to Madras and Bombay, not becauſe it ſignifies a ſtraw *to Bengal* in whoſe hands thoſe places are, but becauſe their preſervation is thought *neceſſary* for the preſervation *of the Britiſh intereſts in India.*

With

With fuch drains, continued for fuch a fe-
ries of years, with every channel that for-
merly fupplied Bengal with wealth dried up,
is it extraordinary that the mafs of the people, thofe who refide in great towns excepted,
are advancing haftily to poverty and wretchednefs? The wonder is, that a fingle rupee
is left in the country. It convinces us, however, of this truth, that notwithftanding the
refearches of the wifeft men, and the foundeft
politicians, wealth will find its way into a
country through channels imperceptible to
the niceft obferver. We all of us know the
immenfe fums that have been fent from Bengal in the Britifh adminiftration; but none
of us can divine from whence it has received
a fupply fufficient to anfwer thofe drains.

The next point for confideration is, does
the plan of a *permanent fettlement* hold out a
fair profpect of additional relief? Moft certainly it does not. In the firft place, the
plan of a ten years fettlement *is not yet
adopted*; and when it fhall be adopted, it is
not propofed to *raife the rents at all*; therefore to this country *no* advantage will refult

E   either

either from the ten years fettlement, or the *permanent* place; fhould the latter at any time take place,

Every Englifhman will agree with Lord Cornwallis, that it is our duty to govern Bengal as well as we can, and to make the people as happy as we can.

To effect this defirable point, we are now going to alter the whole tenure of landed property in Bengal; that is to fay, we are going to let the lands for ten years, with a declaration to each renter, that if he pays his rents regularly, they fhall be held for *ever* upon the fame terms, which is in fact, giving to Bengal a new conftitution. It is fuppofed that by this plan property will be better fecured, children will be better educated, the poor will feel poverty and wretchednefs in a lefs degree than they do now, and that a *gradation of ranks*, which his Lordfhip fo anxioufly looks for, will be eftablifhed.

I do not believe it poffible that by any arrangement we may form, we can alter the

nature

nature of the people of Bengal; they ever have been, and ever will be, divided into two claffes, very rich, and miferably poor; I mean the Hindoos. From the nature of our government, we have effectually deftroyed the Mahometan nobility, and country gentlemen; and if we were to re-eftablifh them, they would foon find out how abfurd it was, that a great kingdom, with *regular gradations of rank* in it, and inhabited by eighteen millions of people, fhould be governed by a few thoufand men, from a diftant quarter of the globe.

Lord Cornwallis looks to a future increafe of wealth from additional *duties* on the *neceffaries* and *luxuries* of life. In the propriety of Mr. Francis's remarks upon this paragraph I entirely concur.

All revenues are paid by the mafs of the people, and *their* luxuries in Bengal are rice, falt, beetle nut, tobacco, and fifh, with which the rivers abound. It were earneftly to be wifhed that *all* internal duties were totally abolifhed; they are vexatious and oppreffive

in

in the higheſt degree. My own opinion is
very ſtrongly confirmed upon this ſubjeƈt by
that of a gentleman whoſe knowledge, abi-
lity, and candour cannot be diſputed. He
ſays, in a letter written laſt year that I have
lately ſeen; " For my own part, ſo perſuaded
" am I of the difficulty of preventing undue
" exaƈtion in the collection of duties, from
" my experience in this branch of buſineſs,
" where my utmoſt attention to a ſingle
" city did not, I am ſatisfied, prevent it,
" and where numerous, unauthorized extor-
" tions had continued, in defiance of repeat-
" ed prohibitions, in the preſence almoſt of
" the Supreme Government, that if no check
" can be eſtabliſhed to prevent effeƈtually the
" continuance of ſuch impoſitions, and the
" amount realized by Government be not too
" conſiderable to be given up, in the preſent
" exigence of the Company's affairs, I ſhould
" heartily hope the whole collection might
" be aboliſhed," &c. &c.

I am confident that upon further conſidera-
tion, Lord Cornwallis will not look for increaſe of wealth from additional *duties*; they
muſt

muſt from the nature of things be *always* oppreſſive in Bengal, and may ſometimes not defray the expence of the harpies employed in collecting them.

The great ſources of revenue in Bengal are land, and ſalt. As population increaſes, waſte lands will be brought into cultivation, and a fair additional revenue will accrue to Government. As population increaſes, the conſumption of ſalt will increaſe alſo, and Government will acquire an additional revenue on fair terms.

In another part of Lord Cornwallis's Letter, he mentions the ſtate and condition of the Province of Benares, in a manner highly honourable to the gentleman, who has the entire management of that province. The lands have lately been let at a reduced jumma for three years, and although the city of Benares has been annually increaſing ſince the expulſion of Cheyt Sing, the province has materially ſuffered from bad management. The Britiſh government has now taken the collection of the revenues entirely upon itſelf, and there can be no danger of their falling off in future. Of the ftate of Benares, neither Mr. Dundas, nor Mr. Francis faid one word.

They were equally filent as to the ftate and condition of Oude, though the connection between that kingdom and our provinces is of fo peculiar a nature. But though I am as willing as any man to give Lord Cornwallis credit, not only for the beft intentions in the world, but for real and fubftantial public fervices, I muft fay, that however beneficial the arrangements which he has formed may be, they are in various inftances directly contrary to the voice of this nation, proclaimed by its reprefentatives.

That Mr. Dundas fhould have been filent, I am not furprized, becaufe he ftands in the curious predicament of having pointedly condemned in one character, that fyftem which as warmly he has approved in another; but I wonder how it happened that Mr. Francis miffed fo glaring an inconfiftency.

Mr.

Mr. Dundas said, that after what *had hap-pened*, no Governor General would *dare* to depart from the system of *moderation*, which this country had approved. I have already shewn, that in Bengal the system is precisely the same as it has been for years. In Benares, with great propriety, but in direct violation of the rights of the Rajah, Lord Cornwallis has assumed the entire government of the Zemindary. In Oude he has sanctioned and rendered permanent, the system which the House of Commons has condemned, in the strongest possible language. His Lordship has promised his protection to Hyder Beg Khan, the Minister of the sovereign of Oude, as long as he discharges his duty to his master, and pays the subsidy to the Company with regularity. His Lordship has expressed a *hope*, that no occasion will ever occur when he shall be obliged to perform this promise, but upon the faithful performance of it, if necessary, Hyder Beg rests with the utmost confidence.

Not only has Lord Cornwallis *dared* to do this in defiance of the opinion of the House of Com-

Commons, but he has had the magnanimity to ftate it without referve. He has faid, that in his arrangements in Oude, he has nearly adhered to the fyftem laid down by the former Governor General, Mr. Haftings, or where he has made an alteration, it was with a view to render that fyftem *the more permanent.* The fact is, that at the prefent moment, and from the day of Lord Cornwallis's acceffion to the government of Bengal, Hyder Beg Khan has been, in effect, the abfolute fovereign of Oude, with the full knowledge, and avowed approbation of Mr. Dundas; yet, the fame gentleman, as a member of parliament, has called Hyder Beg an *implacable tyrant*; and now joins in profecuting Mr. Haftings before the firft tribunal in the kingdom, for that very Syftem, which Lord Cornwallis takes merit for having rendered *permanent*; and which Mr. Dundas has fanctioned with his complete approbation.

On the fide of Bengal, I look in vain for proof of our *moderation.*

We

We have affumed the entire fovereignty of the country, and the Nabob is a pageant, and a penfioner, *in* the receipt of half the falary that we are bound by a folemn treaty to pay him.

Benares we govern completely, under a refident, who is fubject to the board of revenue in Calcutta. To Hyder Beg Khan we have promifed protection, provided his fovereign either from caprice, or the advice of unworthy favourites, fhould withdraw his confidence from him; and we draw a fubfidy from Oude, which defrays one third of the expence of our whole army. Thefe are proofs of a firm and vigorous government; but to talk of the *moderation* of the Englifh, is to ufe a term perfectly unintelligible.

In the other parts of India, this nation, as in the cafe of America, has found out its error. It was the favourite idea for a long time, that England could not exift without America; and after expending a hundred millions of money, and a hundred thoufand men, we have difcovered that we do better

F   without

without it, than with it, and have now only to lament the loss of so many lives, and the accumulation of such a debt.

It was supposed in England, that it was absolutely necessary to keep a large military force at Bombay; territory upon the continent was eagerly wished for, as the means of paying that force, and for that purpose only; internal disputes amongst the Mahrattas gave to the government of Bombay what they thought a fair opening for the acquisition of dominion—they seized it, and the Directors, under the guidance of his Majesty's ministers, approved their measures; the supreme council thought otherwise, they concluded a peace, which was reprobated at home; the war with America brought on a war with France; every thinking man supposed that India would be the main object with that restless nation; the war with the Mahrattas re-commenced; Hyder's invasion of the Carnatic followed; powerful French armaments arrived in India; and by great good fortune two considerable reinforcements were intercepted near the French ports; for three years we fought in India for our existence;

iftence; at the very crifis of our fate, we effected a feparate peace with the Mahrattas; a
ceffation of hoftilities with France was the
happy confequence of the peace in Europe;
and the agreement with Tippoo reftored tran-
quillity to all India; but did the general return of peace, or has any one tranfaction
fince, impreffed the native Princes of India
with an opinion of our *moderation?* In con-
cluding the war we obtained the beft terms
we could; and the peace will be preferved by
the dread of our arms, and our power; not
from a conviction of our *moderation.* Every
Prince in India will fay, if, with an union of
the four great powers of India, affifted by
the French, we could not fubdue the Englifh,
what can be effected by a fingle fovereign,
when France has withdrawn her forces? It
is this reflection which will preferve peace in
India.

The natives in India are not fo ftupid, as
not to know that Mr. Haftings, to whom Mr.
Dundas alluded, is *not* profecuted, becaufe he
wanted *moderation.* They fee that the very
fame fyftem that he eftablifhed, is continued

F ?   by

by Lord Cornwallis, *in all its parts.* Mr.
Haftings is not accufed of having been thé
author of the Mahratta war; which accele-
rated, if it did not caufe, the invafion of the
Carnatic, and was an additional incitement to
France to turn her attention and her force
to India.

If fuch had been the accufation, though
it had not been proved, Mr. Dundas *might*
with propriety fay, that no Governor General would in future dare to depart from that
fyftem of *moderation,* which the Commons
of England had approved.

I know it was faid in the Houfe of Commons by Mr. Dundas, that he never knew
an inftance of a more flagrant violation of a
folemn treaty, than was committed by the
fupreme Council, on the death of Sujah Dow-
lah; when the prefent Nabob was compelled
to alienate a very valuable part of his heredi-
tary dominions; but the injuftice of the act
was loft in the contemplation of its beneficial
importance to the public, and accordingly
the

the majority of the Council * received the thanks of the Company, for an act which set *moderation* and *justice* at defiance. I know that Mr. Dundas moved a resolution in the House of Commons, condemning the suspension of the payment of the tribute to the Mogul, as violating the conditions upon which we oftensibly hold Bengal at the present moment, but it has never occurred to him to offer the least assistance to that unfortunate Monarch during the five years that the power of India has been in his hands.

In both instances, the English perhaps acted according to the rules of sound policy, but we certainly gave no proofs of our *moderation* in either transaction, nor will *mere professions* of moderation, let them come from what quarter they may, obtain the least credit. In the two political transactions of Lord Cornwallis's government, he has strictly adhered to the system of his predecessor; the first, in his arrangements with the Nabob of Oude; the second, in paying Nizam Ally Cawn, the

* Messrs. Clavering, Monson, and Francis.

Peshcush

Pefhcufh for the northern Circars, and in demanding the ceffion of the guntoor on the death of Bazalet Jung; it would have been fome proof of our *moderation*, but a greater proof of our imbecility, if we had forborne to make the demand, or had not determined to enforce it, provided Tippoo Sultan, as was expected, had oppofed us in getting poffeffion of it.

The fact is, that we have an empire in India large enough to fatisfy the ambition of the proudeft nation upon earth. I do not believe any man entertained an idea of enlarging the empire; but fome additional fecurity was thought neceffary on the weft of India, to counteract the defigns of the French, when Great Britain was overwhelmed by enemies in every quarter of the globe. The power of of France *is no more in India*; and as a proprietor, I look with fome anxiety for the reductions that ought to take place in the large armies now kept up in the Carnatic, and at Bombay. When thefe reductions are made, the debt of India may, I think, be gradually

2   dif-

difcharged in India ; and then the annual neceffity of borrowing in England will ceafe.

    To prove that there is a very fair profpect
of a complete difcharge of the Company's
debt in India, and a fund fufficient for the
purchafe of all the inveftment that can be
difpofed of in Leadenhall Street, I fhall quote
the letter from Lord Cornwallis and his council, of the 12th of March 1789. " We
" have every reafon, from a view of the ag-
" gregate amount of the Bengal refources,
" compared with the probable difburfe-
" ments, to confirm you in the expectation
" of drawing from hence a furplus revenue
" of *more than two crores of rupees.*"

    . This furplus is fixed upon that ftrong au-
thority, that cannot well be difputed. Lord
Cornwallis, with the advantage of three years
refidence, is of that opinion ; fo are his
council. The King's minifters and the directors agree in it alfo. But what, in my judge-
ment is decifive upon the queftion, is this,
that the receipts for a number of years back,
in Bengal, have been fo equal, as to leave
very

very little doubt of their continuance at the fame amount. If there fhould be a difference in future, I am convinced there will be an increafe.

It has been faid, and very naturally, how does it happen, that with fuch a furplus, the Company has been reduced to the neceffity of borrowing fuch large fums of money in England? To thofe, who for one moment will confider the fubject, the caufes are obvious.

In the firft place, the commutation act rendered it neceffary for the Company to double their capital employed in commerce.

Secondly, it happened in India, as in England, that it was impoffible, previous to the conclufion of the war, to know precifely the amount of the military expences at Madras and Bombay; and to this it was owing, not to intentional deception in the Directors, that the accounts prefented to Parliament in 1784, were fo exceedingly defective.

The

The very fame thing happened in England: we never knew the amount of the national debt during Lord North's adminiftration, nor until two years after the clofe of the war.— Bills have been drawn upon the Direction for above two millions beyond their eftimate, fince 1784.

The third caufe of the embarraffed ftate of the Company's affairs at home was, the refolution taken by the Directors, in conjunction with his Majefty's Minifters, to transfer the India debt to Great Britain. Above two millions have been already fubfcribed. I admit, that at the time the refolution paffed, it was wife and proper; but France having withdrawn herfelf from India, and fo clofe a connection having been formed with Holland, I think the remainder of the India debt may be paid abroad.

The fourth caufe of the Company's diftrefs at home was, the confiderable fums paid to Government in the three laft years, for the pay of his Majefty's regiments ferving in India.

G   The

The fifth caufe was, the very large and expenfive military eftablifhments formed for Madras and Bombay. However neceffary thefe might have been, while an opinion prevailed, that France would never fuffer us to be at peace in India, that neceffity, moft happily, exifts no longer. There can be no reafon now, why Bombay fhould not be put upon the fame eftablifhment that exifted twenty years ago, independent of the troops propofed to be fent to Travancore, for which a fubfidy equal to their expence is to be paid. In this event, ten lacks a-year would be fufficient to make up the expences of Bombay, in addition to her own revenue.

At Madras, the eftablifhment may be reduced, fo as to allow a fum to be appropriated for an inveftment, after the payment of its expences. Any addition from Bengal would then be of real importance, becaufe the Madras inveftment fells to a profit in Leadenhall Street.

There is one material confideration which I truft neither the Houfe of Commons as a body,

body; nor the individual members of it, will lofe fight of; when they are deliberating upon the embarraffed ftate of the Company's affairs in England. It is this; that the embarraffment is the effect of the war in India; and the war in India was brought upon the Company by the meafures propofed by the Minifter, and adopted by Parliament.

Mr. Fox's arguments upon this fubject remain to the prefent day unanfwered, and they are unanfwerable. Two years prior to the commencement of hoftilities with France, he foretold a war with that nation as the inevitable confequence of the protraction of the American conteft; and war with France, he truly faid, would involve us in every quarter of the globe. It is of no moment now to inquire, whether in the commencement of the fecond Mahratta war we imputed fchemes to France which at that time fhe had not entertained. The information came from the firft authority, and the Government of Bengal would have been deemed criminal if fuch information had been flighted. " Beware of " the defigns of the French " was the conftant

advice

advice of the Directors to their servants in India, and France probably owes her present ruin to the prodigious exertions which she made in the late war, in order to wrest India from Great Britain. To counteract such exertions, and to break the general confederacy formed against us, required great expences on our part; but if we consider for one moment the relative state of Great Britain and Bengal, the embarrassments of the latter will sink to nothing.

We effected a peace in Europe by acknowledging the independence of America, by the cession of some West-India islands to France, by giving up the Floridas and Minorca to Spain, and by allowing the French a footing in India, to which they were not entitled by their successes in that quarter of the globe. For three years after the peace we were borrowing money, and imposing new taxes, in order to defray the expences of the war, and we doubled the national debt.

In Bengal, which furnished such immense supplies for the support of the war, without the
impo-

impofition of one additional tax, (and taxes there upon an European fyftem are un-known) we have a furplus of more than two millions fterling a-year. The debt of India had long ago been paid off if this furplus had been appropriated to that purpofe ; but a con-viction of the immenfe importance of India to Great Britain, and the recollection of the efforts which France made in the late war to deprive us of it, induced the King's Minifters to guard us effectually againft their future attempts; and they fixed the military efta-blifhments fo high, as not only to abforb all the favings that were made in the civil and revenue departments, but to require in addition the remittance of confiderable fums from Bengal to Madras and Bombay.

After all that has been faid of the *œco-nomical arrangements* of the Board of Con-troul, I fancy I fhall hardly obtain credit for the following ftatement ; but I will refer my readers to authorities that cannot miflead them.

The

The total expences of India the year preceding the late war, that is, from April 1777 to April 1778, amounted to £3,387,727.

The total expences of India for 1788-9 £5,053,997.

I have taken the firſt ſtatement from papers publiſhed in the Sixth Report of the Secret Committee, (Mr. Dundas's) and the latter from the papers preſented this year to the Houſe of Commons on the motion of Mr. Dundas. When I ſpeak of India, I mean Bengal, Fort St. George, and Bombay.— Should there be any inaccuracy, it is too trifling to be worth notice, and admitting that the whole expence attending the Collections in Bengal in the firſt period is not included, I can ſafely affirm, that after all the boaſted reductions, the expences of 1788-9, when we have not the moſt diſtant proſpect of war, exceed the expences of 1777-8, when a war was inevitable, above one million five hundred thouſand pounds, and of this ſum ſix hundred and

ſeventy

seventy thousand eight hundred and sixty-one pounds is the excess of expence at Madras and Bombay last year, beyond the establishments of 1777-8. These are the establishments to be reformed; but the revenues and resources of Bengal have increased in a proportion infinitely beyond the expences incurred, nor do I conceive that they can be reduced below their present standard.

A dread of French power and French intrigues induced us to send four regiments to India two years ago: both are now at an end; it follows, of course, that reductions to a very considerable amount may safely be ordered. In close alliance with Holland, and the contest given up by France, what can Great Britain have to fear in India?

Except very considerable reductions take place at Madras and Bombay, and unless the debt of India be paid in India, Mr. Dundas may come forward annually to the House of Commons with the same flattering accounts of the Bengal surplus; but he will have also to present each year a petition from the Directors,

rectors, praying further affiftance from Parliament ; and the only advantage we fhall derive from India, will be, that while we retain it, it will be a fruitful fource of patronage to his Majefty's Minifters, and to the Directors of the Eaft India Company.

F I N I S.

www.ingramcontent.com/pod-product-compliance
Lightning Source LLC
Chambersburg PA
CBHW021552270326
41931CB00009B/1174